Marx Joyce Abbott Hardy Montaigne Machiavelli Chesterton Cooper Emerson Austen Defoe Melville Haggard Hugo Eliot Grimm Stoker Carroll Christie Molière Wilde Maupassant Byron Schiller Engels Garnett Einstein Fitzgerald Hawthorne Smith Kafka Goethe Dostoyevsky Cotton Hall Baum Kipling Doyle Willis Leslie Dumas Henry Nietzsche Flaubert Turgenev Balzac Stockton Vatsyayana Crane Burroughs Verne Curtis Tocqueville Whitman Gogol Vinci Homer Widger Tolstoy Busch Darwin Thoreau Potter Freud Zola Twain Plato Scott Lawrence Kant Jowett Stevenson Dickens Andersen Burton Hesse Harte London Descartes Cervantes Poe Aristotle Wells Voltaire Hale James Hastings Cooke Bunner Shakespeare Richter Chambers Irving Doré Swift Dante Chekhov da Shaw Wodehouse Benedict Alcott Pushkin Newton tredition®

tredition was established in 2006 by Sandra Latusseck and Soenke Schulz. Based in Hamburg, Germany, tredition offers publishing solutions to authors and publishing houses, combined with worldwide distribution of printed and digital book content. tredition is uniquely positioned to enable authors and publishing houses to create books on their own terms and without conventional manufacturing risks.

For more information please visit: www.tredition.com

TREDITION CLASSICS

This book is part of the TREDITION CLASSICS series. The creators of this series are united by passion for literature and driven by the intention of making all public domain books available in printed format again - worldwide. Most TREDITION CLASSICS titles have been out of print and off the bookstore shelves for decades. At tredition we believe that a great book never goes out of style and that its value is eternal. Several mostly non-profit literature projects provide content to tredition. To support their good work, tredition donates a portion of the proceeds from each sold copy. As a reader of a TREDITION CLASSICS book, you support our mission to save many of the amazing works of world literature from oblivion. See all available books at www.tredition.com.

Project Gutenberg

The content for this book has been graciously provided by Project Gutenberg. Project Gutenberg is a non-profit organization founded by Michael Hart in 1971 at the University of Illinois. The mission of Project Gutenberg is simple: To encourage the creation and distribution of eBooks. Project Gutenberg is the first and largest collection of public domain eBooks.

Peter Cooper The Riverside Biographical Series, Number 4

Rossiter W. (Rossiter Worthington) Raymond

Imprint

This book is part of TREDITION CLASSICS

Author: Rossiter W. (Rossiter Worthington) Raymond
Cover design: Buchgut, Berlin – Germany

Publisher: tredition GmbH, Hamburg - Germany
ISBN: 978-3-8472-1301-7

www.tredition.com
www.tredition.de

The intention of the TREDITION CLASSICS series is to make world literature in the public domain available in printed format. Literary enthusiasts and organizations, such as Project Gutenberg, worldwide have scanned and digitally edited the original texts. tredition has subsequently formatted and redesigned the content into a modern reading layout. Therefore, we cannot guarantee the exact reproduction of the original format of a particular historic edition. Please also note that no modifications have been made to the spelling, therefore it may differ from the orthography used today.

The Riverside Biographical Series

NUMBER 4

PETER COOPER

BY

ROSSITER W. RAYMOND

[ii]

The Riverside Biographical Series

1. ANDREW JACKSON, by W. G. Brown.
2. JAMES B. EADS, by Louis How.
3. BENJAMIN FRANKLIN, by Paul E. More.
4. PETER COOPER, by R. W. Raymond.
5. THOMAS JEFFERSON, by H. C. Merwin.
6. WILLIAM PENN, by George Hodges.
7. GENERAL GRANT, by Walter Allen.
8. LEWIS AND CLARK, by William R. Lighton.
9. JOHN MARSHALL, by James B. Thayer.
10. ALEXANDER HAMILTON, by Chas. A. Conant.
11. WASHINGTON IRVING, by H. W. Boynton.
12. PAUL JONES, by Hutchins Hapgood.
13. STEPHEN A. DOUGLAS, by W. G. Brown.
14. SAMUEL DE CHAMPLAIN, by H. D. Sedgwick, Jr.

Each about 140 pages, 16mo, with photogravure portrait, 65 cents, *net; School Edition*, each, 50 cents, *net*.

HOUGHTON MIFFLIN COMPANY
Boston and New York

[iv]

Peter Cooper

PETER COOPER

BY

ROSSITER W. RAYMOND

BOSTON AND NEW YORK
HOUGHTON MIFFLIN COMPANY
The Riverside Press Cambridge

[v]

[vi]

PREFACE

During the last decade of Peter Cooper's life, the writer of this biographical sketch enjoyed some degree of intimacy with him, as professional adviser and traveling companion, and also, incidentally, as consulting engineer of the firm of Cooper and Hewitt, and manager of a department in the Cooper Union. This circumstance, together with the preference kindly expressed by Mr. Cooper's family, doubtless influenced the selection of the writer for the honorable task of preparing this book,—a task which was welcome as a labor of love, though the execution of it has been hindered and impaired by the demands of other duties. The real difficulty has been to compress within the prescribed limits a story covering so many years and so many topics, yet not possessing those features of dramatic action or adventure which could be treated briefly, with picturesque effect. [viii]

Mr. Cooper's family has kindly furnished abundant material for this work, including, besides his own published utterances, the notes of the stenographer to whom Mr. Cooper, in the last years of his life, dictated his "reminiscences." The use which has been made of these will be evident to the reader. Beyond an occasional revelation of the character of the speaker, or a side-light thrown upon the manners and conditions of our early national life, they have not furnished valuable data; and the study of them suggests an observation which may be heeded with advantage in similar cases hereafter, though it comes too late to be useful in this instance, namely, that the recollections of old people with retentive memories, like Peter Cooper, may be invaluable, if they are intelligently aroused and guided; but if the speakers (as in his case) are left to their own initiative, they are too likely to furnish superfluous accounts of events already described more accurately in authentic contemporaneous records.

It has not been practicable to preserve, [ix] in the treatment of the subject, a strictly chronological order. As the titles of the several chapters indicate, the different lines of Mr. Cooper's activity have been considered, to some extent, separately, so that their periods overlap each other.

This sketch of Mr. Cooper's career furnishes the elements of an analysis, which I introduce here, as a guide in the interpretation of what is to follow.

1. The time of his birth and the prophetic anticipations of his parents profoundly influenced his ambition to do something great for his fellow-citizens of the republic whose life began so nearly with his own.

2. The atmosphere surrounding his youth was one of unlimited and audacious adventure. New institutions, a virgin continent, the ardent desire to be independent of the Old World, and a profound belief in the destiny of America, all combined to stimulate endeavor. What Peter Cooper said of himself as an apprentice was true of the typical young American of his time: "I was always [x] planning and contriving, and was never satisfied unless I was doing something difficult—something that had never been done before, if possible."

3. The new freedom and the vast opportunity presented in the young republic encouraged, to a degree not paralleled before or since, that change of occupation which, with all its drawbacks, had the one great merit that it educated men to various activities. It was no disgrace to an American to go into one business after another, seeking the one which would prove most profitable and agreeable. Thus, Peter Cooper worked successively as a hatter, a coach-builder, a machinist, a machine-maker, a grocer, an iron-worker, and a glue-manufacturer, achieving success in every occupation, but abandoning each for something more promising, and learning in each something which promoted his success in the next.

4. At every stage of his progress, he followed the ideal of personal independence, the honest acquisition of property, the establishment of a home, and the rearing of a [xi] family. These were the first duties and the dearest wishes—no matter what greater things might lie beyond. And he profoundly realized that temperance, industry, frugality, and patience were the necessary preliminaries to any longed-for achievement. As he says, he had first to spend thirty years in getting a start; then to spend another thirty years in accumulating the means for further advance into the wider sphere of his aspirations. And during each stage of this process, he was patient, as well as hopeful, neither wasting his energies in visionary

schemes nor allowing the eddies of daily toil to divert the current of his deeper purposes.

5. At every stage, however, he found himself hindered by lack of thorough knowledge. He invented perpetually and profusely; but some of his most cherished inventions did not find practical recognition, because he had attempted the premature or the impossible. His guiding principle, of trying to do something that had never been done before, is not an adequate substitute [xii] for a scientific knowledge of what can be, and now needs to be, done. He found himself often too far in advance of his generation. Moreover, he found that the lack of education crippled him in the attempt to make other men understand and appreciate his fruitful ideas. This is true of all really great "self-made men." They may have achieved success and fame in spite of early disadvantages; they may, perhaps, recognize the fact that such disadvantages, necessitating a stern struggle, have sifted out, by natural selection, the possessors of genius and sterling character; but not one of them fails to lament the lack of that early training which would have made him still more successful than he is; and not one of them fails to desire, for his children and the coming generation of his fellows, the early advantages which were denied to himself.

6. This experience it was which gave form to the aspirations and purposes of Peter Cooper. As an apprentice, he resolved to do something for the benefit of apprentices—to found some institution [xiii] which should supplement the deficiencies of early education, furnishing to virtuous, industrious, and ambitious youths the means of progress, and attracting the thoughtless or indolent into the same ascending road. How this conception came to be both modified and realized will be seen in later pages. At this point it is sufficient to note that the plan was originally not only philanthropic, but patriotic and practical. It contemplated the benefit, through means adapted to their special condition, of Americans of that class to which Peter Cooper himself belonged.

Some further observations concerning the secret of the universal esteem and affection enjoyed by Mr. Cooper will be reserved for the closing chapter. [1]

PETER COOPER

I

ANCESTRY

Obadiah Cooper, who, with his two brothers, came from England to the colony of New York about 1662, belonged, as we may infer with confidence, to that sturdy class of republican yeomanry which found the restored reign of the Stuarts intolerable. He settled at Fishkill-on-the-Hudson; and his son Obadiah—whom tradition declares to have been the fourth white man child born in what is now Dutchess County—was the great-grandfather of Peter Cooper. In 1720 an Obadiah of the next generation followed, and of his son John, born in 1755, Peter Cooper was the fifth child.

John Cooper came of age in the year of the Declaration of Independence. In the [2] issue between the British government and the American colonies his choice could not be doubtful. He followed the traditions of his family. Indeed, it is now well established and universally admitted that the patriots of the American Revolution were not in fact arrayed against England. They were engaged in a struggle which was but a part of the great conflict waged against shortsighted and obstinate tyranny by Englishmen on both sides of the ocean, and in which the victory for liberty was won on this side sooner than on the other. What the Coopers and their kind achieved here was applauded openly in the mother country by the descendants of a common ancestry as a triumph for the common cause. The use of foreign mercenaries under British commanders in this country was the direct result of the impossibility of inducing Englishmen to enlist for service against their American kinsmen. Hence when John Cooper, of Fishkill, abandoned in 1776 the business he had just established as a hatter, and became sergeant in a company of "minute-men," he [3] was but pursuing the course indicated both by his own convictions and by the history of his fathers and the sympathies of the party in England to which they had belonged. It was Freedom's battle "handed down from sire to son."

He served subsequently for two years in the Continental line, and for the last four years of the war as a lieutenant in the New York militia, actively employed in the perilous service of protecting life, property, and the public stores in the zone of debatable territory,—the "bloody ground" which surrounded the British lines in New York. At the close of the war, New York having been evacuated by the enemy, Lieutenant John Cooper retired to civil life, and resumed business as a hatter in that city,—a worthy example of that American citizen soldiery which has always been equally ready to leave the ways of peace for its country's defense, and to return to them when the exigency had passed.

It was in 1779, during his military service, that John Cooper married Margaret, the [4] daughter of John Campbell, a deputy quartermaster-general in the Continental army, and a trusted agent of Washington. The outbreak of hostilities in 1776 had found John Campbell a prosperous merchant and owner of real estate in New York city. He at once lent to the Revolutionary government eleven hundred guineas,—the whole of his ready money,—entered the service, was made deputy quartermaster-general, and was directed to superintend the hasty evacuation of the city by the Whig inhabitants, and to protect them and their property as far as possible. Lingering too long to assist some of the laggards, he was captured by the forces landed from the British fleet, but was subsequently released; and he made a temporary home at Fishkill while actively engaged in establishing the lines by which the British army, though holding the city and commanding its access to the sea, was practically besieged. General Campbell served throughout the war, and after hostilities had ceased commanded the troops at West Point until they were finally disbanded in 1785. [5]

It is easy to imagine how the young lieutenant and the daughter of the commander who must have been frequently brought into personal relations with him may have met and loved and wedded in the midst of those troublous times, but the romance would have no special bearing on this history. It is enough to say that by this marriage the best blood of England and Scotland—of servants of God and lovers of freedom—was blended in the nine children, seven sons and two daughters, of whom Peter Cooper—born February

12, 1791, in Little Dock (now Water) Street, New York—was the fifth.

John Cooper was not characteristically a seer of visions or a dreamer of dreams. On the contrary, the accounts of him which have come down to us describe him as a stalwart athlete, who "could lift a barrel of cider from the ground and put it in a wagon," and who once, being cornered and attacked by a bull, seized the animal's nose with one hand and so battered its head with a stone that it was glad to turn and fly. [6] Yet he came of a race that believed in Divine guidance; and on one occasion at least he acted upon that belief in a matter then deemed more important, perhaps, than now. The incident can be given best in the words of Peter Cooper himself, who wrote:—

"My father used to tell me how he came to call me Peter. When I was born he became strongly impressed with the idea that I would some day have more than ordinary fame, and what name he should give me was a matter of serious and frequent thought. While walking on Broadway one dark night it seemed as though a voice spoke to him in a clear and distinct manner: 'Call him Peter!' That seeming voice settled my name. My father said that he felt that I was to be of great good in some way; and his remarks, with my mother's, concerning their aspirations and hopes for me acted as a stimulus and made me anxious to fulfill their wishes, and not disappoint them."

If names were to be characteristic of individual careers, it might be better to imitate some Indian tribes, and to give the permanent [7] name only after the career, or at least the character, of its recipient had been indicated by his acts. In this instance the subsequent life of the son did not in any peculiar way imitate that of the Apostle Peter. Evidently not that particular name, but the simple fact that an eminent name, thus suggested and not already familiar in his family, had been given to him, produced upon his mind the effect to which he testifies.

But why should practical John Cooper be disposed to anticipate a special distinction for the infant who was the fifth of his numerous progeny? From the standpoint of the modes of thought of the godly patriots of that generation, and of their ancestors, the English Puritans and the Scotch Covenanters, it is scarcely hazardous to assume that current public affairs largely affected such domestic choices. Peter Cooper's birth was practically simultaneous with the launching of that Ship of State, the "Union, strong and great," in which all patriots had embarked "their hopes, triumphant o'er their [8] fears." To his veteran-soldier father he was the first child of the new era; and the dreams that were dreamed over him were doubtless connected with that glorious future which had just dawned upon the federated republic. The choice of an unfamiliar, non-hereditary name, however suggested, symbolized the break between the old time and the new.

Above all, this incident produced in the son thus christened the profoundest effects, the deepest motives, that can inspire a boyish soul,—the belief in a beneficent mission, the yearning to discover it, the resolve to execute it, and the conviction that it was to be directly connected with the prosperity and progress of the great nation, the life of which began with his own.

The naming of Peter Cooper thus strikes the keynote, or, more accurately, the triple chord, of his life. For he was first of all an American, keenly aware of the opportunities offered by the free institutions of his country to individual ambition, industry, and genius, and of his own personal ability to [9] make use of these opportunities. Secondly, he was a lover of his fellow men, determined to employ for their benefit the means and powers which he felt himself able to accumulate by thought, toil, and frugal economy. Thirdly, he was even in his philanthropy essentially still an American, intent most of all upon the welfare of those classes of his countrymen with whose struggles and needs his own early life had made him familiar. In other words, while his philanthropy covered a world-wide range, his peculiar mission, as he conceived it, was indissolubly blent with the success of the republic of which he was one of the earliest-born sons.

[10]

II

BOYHOOD AND YOUTH

At a meeting of friends, gathered February 12, 1882, to celebrate his ninety-first birthday anniversary, Mr. Cooper, after expressing his thanks for their congratulatory good wishes, and observing that in his case "length of days had not yet resulted in weariness of spirit," added this review of his life:—

"Looking back, I can see that my career has been divided into three eras. During the first thirty years I was engaged in getting a start in life; during the second thirty years I was occupied in getting means for carrying out the modest plan which I had long formed for the benefit of my fellow men; and during the last thirty years I have devoted myself to the execution of these plans. This work is now done."

Accepting this division of his career, as convenient, though not strictly accurate [11] (since the processes described really overlapped instead of separately succeeding one another), we may consider first Mr. Cooper's means and method of achieving personal success; and in this survey the conditions of his boyhood and early youth are primarily important.

While he was still very young, the family removed from a temporary residence of three years in New York city to Peekskill, where he remained until, at the age of seventeen, he returned to New York as an apprentice, to be, thenceforward, dependent upon his own exertions for a living.

The intervening period was spent in ways characteristic of the period and of the individual. He attended school for three or four "quarters," of which period, according to his later recollection, "probably half was occupied by 'half-day' school." Outside of this scanty formal instruction, there is ample evidence that he developed body and mind in varied work and play. He bore to the end of life the scars of youthful escapades, witnessing the adventurous spirit of [12] his boyhood. When only four years old, he climbed about the framework of a new house, and fell, head downward, upon an iron kettle, cutting his forehead to the bone. Later on, he was accidentally cut with a knife in the hands of a playmate. Later still, he cut himself dangerously with an axe. Again, he fell from a high tree, holding an iron hook with which he had been reaching for cherry-bearing branches, and managed to hook out one of his teeth. At another time he went for the nest of a hanging-bird, and had the fact that it was a hornet's nest indelibly impressed on his memory. Of course, he was nearly drowned three times,—such youngsters always have such escapes. In short, he was a thorough boy, adventuring all things, daunted by nothing, and protected from the results of his reckless endeavors by that Providence which watches over small boys.

But such a temperament finds play in useful work also. The boy learned every department of the hat-making business, beginning, when he was very young, with pulling [13] the fur from the skins of rabbits. And, while assisting his mother in doing the family washing, he made what was, perhaps, his first invention,—a mechanical arrangement for pounding the soiled linen. Again, after carefully dissecting an old shoe, to learn how it was put together, he determined to make shoes and slippers for the family, and succeeded in turning out products of manufacture which were said to be as good as those to be found, at that day, in the regular trade.

He constructed a toy wagon, sold it for six dollars, managed to gather four dollars more, invested the ten dollars in lottery tickets, and drew only blanks, of which experience he said many years later, "I consider it one of the best investments of my life; for I then learned that it was not my *forte* to make money at games of chance."

When he was between thirteen and fourteen years old, his father built a large malt-house at Newburg, and the son loaded with his own hands and carted to the site selected all the stone for the building. Collecting [14] wild honey and shooting game in the forests around Peekskill were additional employments which combined pleasure with profit. But this life did not satisfy the ambition of the youth; and in 1808, at the age of seventeen, he left the paternal roof and apprenticed himself for four years to John Woodward, a leading coach-builder in New York, whose shop was located on the corner of Broadway and Chambers Street, then the northerly edge of the city, opposite a vegetable garden, the remnants of which, after the occupation of a large portion by city, county, and national buildings, now constitute the City Hall Park. The terms of his employment were his board and a salary of twenty-five dollars a year,—out of which he managed not only to pay all obligations, but also to lay by a little money. During this period he not only mastered the details of the trade, but learned in his hours of leisure other branches, such as ornamental wood-carving, and made several inventions, one of which was a machine for mortising hubs,—an operation performed by hand up to that [15] time. Another invention over which the young apprentice dreamed, and of which he laboriously constructed a model, was an apparatus for utilizing, in the running of machinery, the swift current of the tide in the East River.

[16]

III

BUSINESS VENTURES

At the end of his apprenticeship, his employer offered to set him up in business as a coach-builder, lending him the necessary capital. Many years later, Mr. Cooper told the story thus:—

"I was about to accept his generous offer, when an incident occurred which changed my decision. Mr. Woodward had just completed one of the finest coaches ever built in New York, for a gentleman who was supposed to be one of the richest men in the city. But a day or two before the coach was to be delivered the gentleman died, and it was then found that he was insolvent. This made me hesitate. If I should accept my employer's kind offer and have such a misfortune happen to me in the sale of an elegant and expensive coach, I should consider myself a slave for life, since the law of [17] imprisonment for debt had not then been abolished. So I changed my plans, and went to Hempstead, Long Island, to visit my brother."

The visit to Hempstead became a prolonged residence. He obtained work at $1.50 a day (then regarded as high wages) in a factory making machines for shearing cloth, and after nearly three years had saved enough money to purchase the right for the State of New York to a patented machine for that purpose. He used to tell, in his old age, of his elation when he effected his first sale of a county-right, for which he received five hundred dollars from Mr. Vassar, of Poughkeepsie, afterwards the founder of Vassar College.

The manufacture and sale of the new shearing-machine, into which Mr. Cooper introduced many additional improvements, was a prosperous business, especially during the war of 1812, when domestic woolen goods were in great demand. He married, December 18, 1813, Sarah Bedell, a lady of Huguenot descent, who made for him a happy [18] home during fifty-seven years. [1] He bought a house in Hempstead, expecting to remain there; and in the household, as in business, he gave rein to his ardent and versatile inventive faculty. One of his domestic contrivances rocked the cradle, fanned away the flies, and played a lullaby to the baby. He sold the patent in Connecticut to a Yankee peddler for a horse and wagon, and the peddler's stock, including a hurdy-gurdy. Another invention was a machine for mowing grass, constructed on the principle of his cloth-shearing machine.

But after the war, the domestic woolen mills were shut down, and there was no sale [19] for Mr. Cooper's machines. So he first turned his factory into a furniture shop, and then, selling it for what he could get, he moved to New York, and started in the grocery business, buying for this purpose a long lease of the ground where the Bible House now stands, opposite the Cooper Union on Ninth Street. Upon this ground he erected several buildings, one of which he used as his office. The business was profitable; but the real foundation of Mr. Cooper's wealth was laid when, at the age of thirty-three, he purchased a glue factory, situated where the Park Avenue Hotel now stands, and established himself as a glue manufacturer. The business speedily acquired and held for half a century practically the whole trade of the country in glue and isinglass,—a monopoly fairly earned by the cheapness and excellence of its product.

Mr. Cooper's inventions improved the quality and reduced the cost of his product, while his energy, industry, and frugality steadily increased his surplus cash, and enabled him, without borrowing capital, to [20] extend his sphere of operations. For many years, he carried on his glue business without bookkeeper, agent, or salesman. Dawn found him at the suburban factory (on what is now Thirty-Second Street) lighting the fires and preparing for the day's work; at noon, he drove in his buggy to the city, where he made his own sales and purchases; and all his evenings he spent at home, making up his accounts, answering his correspondents, studying out new inventions, or talking and reading to his wife and children.

By these simple, old-fashioned methods he built up a business and accumulated a fortune too large to be thus administered. It would have been impossible for one head to carry the details of work and management, for one pair of eyes to superintend each part of the work, or for one pair of feet, however tireless, to travel all the ways which lead to and from a great modern industrial establishment. Still less could financial direction and protection be compassed by the simple scheme which Mr. Cooper, in his old age, recalled with pride. "I used," he said once, "to pay all my [21] debts every Saturday night; and I knew that what I had left was my own!" This could not have been strictly true; but it doubtless expressed an old man's memory of the way he began, and the principles he had followed, with that horror of debt which dated from the time when debtors could be put in jail. Fortunately for Mr. Cooper, his son Edward, and his son-in-law, Abram S. Hewitt, were at hand to undertake the management of his business enterprises at the time when his own simple methods would have proved inadequate, so that his inventive genius, adventurous courage, and, above all, intense philanthropy, were backed with ample means.

In this account of his business ventures (though of much later date than those already mentioned) the part played by Peter Cooper in the development of the American iron industry and in the construction of the first transatlantic submarine telegraph may be recorded.

The manufacture of iron was one of the early industries of the American colonies, [22] and after the Revolution it was prosecuted with increased activity in small and primitive establishments. With its development into scientific forms on a large scale Mr. Cooper was both directly and indirectly connected. His Ringwood estate in New Jersey had been the scene of the operations of the Ringwood Company in 1740, and of its successors,—Hasenclever (1764) and Erskine (1771); and the Durham furnace, on the Delaware River in Pennsylvania (on the site of the Durham Iron Works of Cooper &

Hewitt), made its first blast in 1727. Mr. Cooper himself was engaged in 1830 in the manufacture of charcoal iron near Baltimore, and in 1836, together with his brother Thomas, he operated a rolling-mill in New York (on Thirty-Third Street, near Third Avenue). At this mill anthracite was used for puddling in 1840. In 1845 the business was removed to Trenton, N. J.; and in the new rolling-mill—then the largest in the United States—built at Trenton for the manufacture of rails, the first iron beams for buildings were rolled in 1854. By the [23] erection of blast furnaces at Phillipsburg and Ringwood, N. J., and Durham, Pa., and the addition of wire mills, bridge shop, chain shop, etc., to the works at Trenton, the purchase of iron and coal lands, and the development of numerous mines, the firm of Cooper & Hewitt achieved high rank among the ironmasters of America; and the Iron and Steel Institute of Great Britain conferred upon Peter Cooper in 1879 the "Bessemer gold medal" for his services in the development of the American iron trade. In 1890 the same honor was given to Mr. Abram S. Hewitt in recognition of the experiments at Phillipsburg as early as 1856 to test the new invention of Bessemer, of his introduction of the open-hearth steel process into the United States, and of other services rendered to the steel industry,—in all of which he may be said to have followed, with the advantages of a wider culture and ampler means, the example set by Mr. Cooper.

One of the boldest yet wisest and most profitable operations of Mr. Cooper was his investment in the Atlantic cable enterprise [24] of Cyrus Field. He was already past middle age when this audacious scheme began to be dreamed of. In 1842 Morse had laid down an experimental cable from Castle Garden to Governor's Island in New York harbor, and claimed as a practical inference that a telegraphic communication on his plan could "with certainty be established across the Atlantic." [2] In 1851 the first cable was laid between France and England, and others rapidly followed on ocean lines over short distances. The principle was thus established, and the doubts as to its practical application to a line of at least twenty-five hundred miles were of such a character as to seem more serious to scientific men than to American capitalists of Mr. Cooper's type. In March, 1854, the New York, Newfoundland, & London Telegraph Company was organized, and Mr. Cooper became (and remained for twenty trying years) its president. There was little difficulty in raising the money for the eighty-five [25] miles of cable which were to be laid under the Gulf of St. Lawrence, or in obtaining from the British colonies favorable charters granting exclusive privileges, land grants, and even subsidies. Yet the construction of the land line across Newfoundland to the terminus at Heart's Content proved difficult and costly, and the St. Lawrence cable was lost in laying. Yet additional capital was subscribed; and a couple of years later the Newfoundland line, the St. Lawrence cable, and another submarine link of thirteen miles across the Straits of Northumberland had been successfully finished. Nothing remained to be done *except* the procuring of means and the devising of successful methods for the installation of the Atlantic cable itself, without which all this preliminary expenditure would have been thrown away.

The capital estimated as necessary for making and laying the cable was raised by Mr. Field in England, where the Atlantic Telegraph Company was formed to construct and operate the line under concessions from [26] the parent Newfoundland company. All classes in England felt a sentimental interest in the romantic enterprise; and the subscribers to the new stock included such men as Thackeray and others of equal note, outside of business circles altogether.

The company proceeded with vigor,—secured from the governments of Great Britain and the United States guaranties of subsidies and the free use of ships for laying the cable; contracts for the cable and its insulating covering were executed; and by the end of July, 1857, the British Agamemnon and the American Niagara had each twelve hundred and fifty miles of it on board. In August they connected the two halves of it in mid-Atlantic, and in September the shore end was landed at Heart's Content.

The sequel is familiar history. A few messages had been sent and received, when the current grew weaker and weaker, and at last failed entirely. The result was a strong reaction in popular sentiment. It was even questioned whether any messages had actually crossed the Atlantic. Fortunately this doubt [27] could be conclusively disproved,—especially in England, where it was known that the British government had wired by the cable before its failure news of great political importance. The British company indeed courageously proceeded to make another cable; but when this parted in mid-ocean during the process of laying it even British tenacity of purpose was daunted, and for some two years the enterprise seemed to be dead. Meanwhile public opinion on this side was far more unfavorable, and the parent company found itself without means or credit. To retain its privileges it must pay additional money, and to make those privileges worth anything capital must be raised for a third attempt to lay the transatlantic line.

Without describing in detail the difficulties and anxieties of this period, it may be said that the intelligent courage of Peter Cooper saved the enterprise, while it secured to him a large pecuniary reward; for he perceived that the real problem had been solved by the first apparent failure; that [28] the failure of a cable in use or the loss of a cable in laying it were mere incidental misfortunes which more thorough precautions and better luck would preclude; and he backed with his own faith and money the undaunted enthusiasm and persuasive eloquence of Mr. Field, whose expenses he paid for another journey to England, and who succeeded at last in raising there the funds for the third and successful attempt. Moreover Mr. Cooper upheld the credit of the Newfoundland company, personally paying the drafts drawn upon it, and taking its bonds as his security. It is too much to say that the Atlantic cable would never have been laid, but there can be no doubt that the enterprise would have been long suspended, without this timely aid. The third cable was a success; the lost second was recovered and made useful; and now the thing is easy which thus seemed so problematical. If Peter Cooper received in the end a handsome sum from this investment, who could grudge him the wealth so acquired?

[29]

IV

INVENTIONS

The inventions projected, though in many instances not perfected or successfully introduced, by Mr. Cooper constitute a long list and cover a wide field. A few of them may be mentioned here, in addition to those to which allusion has been made already. It will be seen that even those which failed of commercial success generally contained the germs of future mechanical progress, and bore witness to the extraordinary vigor and versatility of his genius.

When the Erie Canal was approaching completion it occurred to Mr. Cooper that canal boats might be propelled by the power of water drawn from a higher level and moving a series of endless chains along the canal. After some preliminary experiments he built a flat-bottomed scow, arranged a water wheel to utilize the tidal current in [30] the East River, and actually achieved a trial trip of two miles and return, in which Governor Clinton and other invited guests took part. The governor was so well pleased that he paid Mr. Cooper eight hundred dollars for the first chance to purchase the right of applying the method on the new canal. But the scheme failed for the reason (as Mr. Cooper explained half a century later) that the right of way for the Erie Canal had been secured from the farmers of the State by representing to them the profit which they would realize from selling forage, etc., for the use of canal boats, which were to be drawn by horses or mules. The introduction of mechanical power would destroy these inducements, and the plan was abandoned,—though Mr. Cooper had demonstrated its feasibility by running his endless chain on the East River for ten days and carrying hundreds of passengers over the trial route. It is not likely that such a use of water power on the Erie Canal would have proved practicable on a large scale; but the endless chain, which Mr. Cooper [31] apparently considered as a minor feature only, has been adopted since, and lies at the basis of the famous Belgian system of river and canal transportation.

In 1824 the wave of enthusiastic sympathy for the Greeks which swept over the country upon receipt of the tidings of their revolt against Turkish tyranny stimulated Mr. Cooper to invent a torpedo boat, to be steered from the shore by "two steel wires, like the reins of a horse." But on the trial trip of the boat a ship crossed and broke the wires when about six of their total length of ten miles had been let out. The delay made the invention too late for use by the Greeks, and it was not further pursued.

About 1835 the subject of aerial navigation had in the United States one of its periodical revivals. Mr. Cooper, believing that a motive power developed from materials of small weight was essential to the solution of the problem, resolved to employ the explosive force of chloride of nitrogen,—one of the most dangerous compounds known to chemists. The result of his experiments in [32] this direction was an explosion which blew his apparatus to pieces, and nearly cost the audacious inventor an eye. In fact, though the organ was saved from total destruction, it was permanently injured.

The conveyance of freight by aerial cables—a method now widely used—was practiced by Mr. Cooper at an early day. The use of elevators in buildings was foreseen and provided for by him in the erection of the Cooper Union building, and in that building also he introduced for the first time iron beams as part of a fire-proof construction. In these and other inventions his prophetic intuitions were illustrated.

But such intuitions do not fully take the place of scientific training; and one of the inventions of Peter Cooper—which he considered for many years, and possibly to the very last, as his crowning achievement—was a curious example of misdirected ingenuity. It is worthy of notice here, however, for another reason, namely, because of its accidental association with one of its inventor's most remarkable triumphs. [33]

As a young apprentice he had studied the steam engine, and had resolved that he would improve it by doing away with the crank. To his mind this was a source of great loss of power, and he believed that, if he could transform the rectilinear motion of the piston rod directly into rotary motion without the intervention of the crank, he would effect a notable economy.

Now, there is no such loss of power through the crank as he imagined, nor is it likely that any other device for obtaining rotary from rectilinear motion will be found superior to that which Watt devised. But Peter Cooper assailed this fancied evil with undoubting confidence, both as to its existence and as to his ability to do away with it. The result was an invention for which he received, April 28, 1828, letters patent of the United States. At that early day patents were comparatively few,—so few that this one bears no number; and the duties of general administration did not prevent the highest officials from attending to details. This patent, issued to Peter Cooper, of New York, [34] was personally signed by John Quincy Adams, President; countersigned by Henry Clay, Secretary of State; transmitted to William Wirt, Attorney-General; examined, approved, and signed by him, and returned to the Department of State for final delivery to the patentee. It grants for fourteen years to the said Peter Cooper, his heirs, administrators, and assignees the exclusive right to make, use, or license others to use, the described improvement in the method of effecting rotary motion directly from the alternate rectilinear motion of a steam piston. Evidently these distinguished statesmen—Adams, Clay, and Wirt—were not experts in mechanics, or at least did not undertake to hinder by technical criticism the experiments of American ambition; and there was no trained corps of patent-examiners to decide upon the novelty, practicability, and usefulness of any proposed improvement in the arts. Probably the government shared at that time the dominant American feeling of unconquerable youth, ready to attack all problems, especially those which previous [35] experience had pronounced insoluble, and to determine the impossible by attempting it. This spirit has in fact more or less dominated the United States Patent Office down to the present time. With all its present equipment of examiners, trained in theory and versed in technical literature, it still concerns itself chiefly in the consideration of a proposed invention with the question of novelty, rather than that of feasibility or value; and the effect has been that, while thousands of patents are granted for absurd, unnecessary, or inoperative devices, the net result of the encouragement thus given to individual ingenuity and audacity is a catalogue of great inventions unmatched in the history of any other nation.

The patent of Peter Cooper, which now lies before me,—a time-stained parchment bearing the great seal of the United States and the autographs of the famous men named above,—is accompanied by no drawings; but it contains a detailed specification which shows that the invention consisted in an arrangement by which, at each forward movement, [36] a prolongation of the piston rod clawed into an endless chain, which was pulled back by the return stroke.

This chain passed around a wheel, to which it consequently imparted a rotary motion.

Engineers do not need to be told that this cumbrous arrangement could not successfully replace the crank, even if such a replacement were desirable. Yet the inventor constructed a working-machine, and satisfied himself, by a "duty trial" of some sort, that it "saved two fifths of the steam." His discovery, however, was not hailed with immediate recognition by the mechanical public; and its author, undisturbed in his faith, bided his time.

This, by the way, points to a characteristic of Peter Cooper, differentiating him from the numerous enthusiasts whom prudent men are accustomed to avoid. He was not a man "of one idea." His fertile and ingenious mind threw out its suggestions in every direction, into fields untrodden by experience; but when any such plan failed of acceptance, he turned, with undiminished [37] courage and hope, to something else, remaining, nevertheless, still steadfast in his former conception, and ready to seize any opportunity for its realization.

Thus it came to pass that Mr. Cooper's abortive improvement upon the steam engine was the source of his fame as the builder of the first American locomotive, as the following chapter will explain.

[38]

V

THE TOM THUMB

In the specification of the patent secured in 1828 by Mr. Cooper for an improved steam engine, he took pains to declare the suitability of his invention as a motor for "land carriages." No doubt he had heard of Stephenson's "Rocket," if not of the engine built by Blenkinsop in 1813, the sight of which in operation caused Stephenson to resolve that he would "make a better." The famous competitive trial of the Rocket, the Novelty, the Sanspareil, and the Perseverance, on a two-mile section of the Liverpool and Manchester Railroad, took place in October, 1827, at which time Peter Cooper must have been perfecting the application for his patent.

But other circumstances played their part in the result which we are about to consider. [39] Some time before 1830 Mr. Cooper had been drawn into a land speculation at Canton, in the suburbs of Baltimore. Failing of support from his partners, he had been obliged to buy them out, and to assume the whole burden of the enterprise. Just at that time there was great popular expectation of the future importance of Baltimore. A little earlier, there had been general despair among the merchants of that city. New York, Philadelphia, and Baltimore were seeking the trade of the region beyond the Alleghanies,—then "the West," but now the centre of the population of the United States. New York flanked the mountains with her Erie Canal; Philadelphia got at last a practicable, though less satisfactory, water line; but Baltimore, though nearest of all to the longed-for market, found, through careful examination by eminent engineers, that no canal was practicable for her, at a cost within her means. In 1824 and 1825 the consequent general despondency concerning the future of the city was [40] so strong that Baltimore merchants began to move to New York and Philadelphia. [3]

But at this period the world began to hear of railways. A well-known merchant of Baltimore, returning from England, described with enthusiasm the coal trains, drawn by the cumbrous ante-Stephenson engines, which he had seen there. The idea of a tramway (with or without steam motors) found ready acceptance in a community both enterprising and desperate. A town meeting, held in 1826, to consider Western communications, resulted in an application to the Maryland legislature, and the incorporation, in March, 1827, of the Baltimore and Ohio,—the first railroad company thus created in the United States for purposes of general transportation,—the leader of that vast multitude of similar enterprises, the history of which is the history of our nation's marvelous commercial progress. [41] By the legislative charter, the city of Baltimore and the State of Maryland were authorized to subscribe to the company's stock.

In the address already cited, Mr. Latrobe, an eye-witness, says of the scenes which followed:—

"Then came a scene which almost beggars description. By this time, public excitement had gone beyond fever heat and reached the boiling point. Everybody wanted stock. The number of shares subscribed were to be apportioned, if the limit of the capital should be exceeded; and every one set about obtaining proxies. Parents subscribed in the names of their children, and paid the dollar on each share that the rules prescribed. Before even a survey had been made, the possession of stock in any quantity was regarded as a provision for old age; and great was the scramble to obtain it. The excitement in Baltimore roused public attention elsewhere; and a railroad mania began to pervade the land."

The proposed railroad was to pass through [42] Mr. Cooper's Canton property, which he had already begun to develop, "so that it should pay the taxes," by building upon it charcoal kilns, after a design of his own, with the purpose of turning the forest into charcoal, and, by means of this fuel, smelting the iron ore which the land contained. What was the immediate commercial outcome of this enterprise is not recorded. Mr. Cooper's characteristic recollection, more than sixty years later, was that, "with the exception of a dangerous explosion," which nearly cost him his life, the charcoal kilns were "a great success!"

But the great value of the property was expected to be realized through the new railroad; and this expectation suffered a serious blow when the horse cars failed to pay expenses; the operation of the line was suspended; the directors lost faith in the enterprise; and many of the principal stockholders declared that they would rather lose the investment made so far than "throw good money after bad." For the hope that the new agency of steam might help them [43] out was blighted by the news from England that Stephenson had said that steam could not be used as a motive power on a road having curves of less than 900 feet radius; and this road had, at Point of Rocks, a necessary curve with a radius of only 150 feet!

The situation presented exactly the sort of challenge calculated to arouse the courage and ingenuity of Peter Cooper, besides appealing to another of his personal characteristics, namely, his undying and unalterable faith in his own ideas and conclusions, whether they had achieved recognition or not. He could lay aside a scheme which had not found immediate and successful application, and turn his attention, with undiminished vivacity, to something else; but he never owned to a real defeat. And now the problem presented at Baltimore seemed to him a providential call for his intervention. If the English engineers could not run their locomotives around sharp curves, it must be because they persisted in using the vicious crank, which he had already superseded by his (temporarily unappreciated) [44] invention! And, with unshaken faith in that device, he informed the Baltimore and Ohio directors (to use the words in which, long afterwards, he told the story) that he thought he "could knock together a locomotive which would get a train around the Point of Rocks."

It is a curious circumstance that, ever since that day, the characteristic difference between English and American locomotives has been the ability of the latter to pass curves of shorter radius than the former can safely follow. The reason, as all railway engineers know, is that the usual English construction involves a rigid frame, while the American has a movable truck or "bogie" under the front part of the engine. This solution of the problem was not reached by Mr. Cooper. What he, in fact, accomplished was simply a piece of audacity, which encouraged the enterprise of his countrymen, by proving that the dictum of limited experience abroad was not conclusive. Two features of his Baltimore experiment were characteristic of him. The first was [45] that he undertook it, not merely in order to vindicate his invention, but to effect a practical result, namely, to make his land speculation pay. And the second was that when he found it difficult to operate his pet invention in this experiment, he laid it aside at once,—without losing an atom of faith in it, but also without persisting (as a typical enthusiast would have done) in risking upon the vindication of his personal opinion in one matter the success of another undertaking, more immediately important.

Mr. Cooper's own recollection of this event deserves to be told in his own words. He says: [4]—

"I came back to New York for a little bit of a brass engine of mine—about one horse power (it had a 3½ in. cylinder and 14 in. stroke)—and carried it back to Baltimore. I got some boiler iron and made a boiler about as high as an ordinary wash boiler; and then how to connect the boiler with the engine I didn't know. I couldn't find any iron pipes. The fact was that [46] there were none for sale in this country. So I took two muskets, broke off the wooden parts, and used the barrels for tubing, one on one side and the other on the other side of the boiler. I went into a coach-maker's shop and made this locomotive, which I called the Tom Thumb, because it was so insignificant. I didn't intend it for actual service, but only to show the directors what could be done. I meant to test two things: first, I meant to show that short turns could be made; and secondly, that I could get rotary motion without the use of a crank. I effected both of these things very nicely. I changed the movement from a reciprocating to a rotary motion.

"I got up steam one Saturday night. The president of the road and two or three other gentlemen were there. We got on the truck and went out two or three miles. All were delighted; for it opened new possibilities for the railroad. I put up the locomotive for the night in a shed, and invited the company to ride to Ellicott's Mills on Monday. Monday morning, what was [47] my chagrin to find that some scamp had been there, and chopped off all the copper from the engine,—doubtless in order to sell it to some junk dealer!

"It took me a week or more to repair the machine; then some one got in and broke a piece out of the wheel, in experimenting with it; and then two wheels, cast one after the other, were damaged by the carelessness of the turner. I was thoroughly disgusted and discouraged; but, being determined that I would not be balked entirely, I changed the engine so that the power could be applied through the ordinary connection with a crank. [5]

"At last all was ready; and, on a Monday, we started,—six in the engine, and thirty-six on the car which I took in tow. We went up an average grade of eighteen feet to the mile; made the thirteen miles to Ellicott's Mills in one hour and twelve minutes; and came back in fifty-seven minutes. [48] The result of that experiment was that the bonds of the railroad company were sold at once, and there was no longer any doubt as to the success of the road."

The Tom Thumb continued for several weeks to make trips to Ellicott's Mills; and on one occasion (September 18, 1830) ran a race from Riley House into Baltimore (about nine miles) with a light car, drawn on a parallel track by a gray horse noted for speed and endurance. The contest was planned by the stagecoach proprietors of Baltimore, with the view of demonstrating that nothing could be gained by the substitution of steam for horse power on the railroad. The gray horse won the race, but not until after the Tom Thumb had passed him, and only by reason of a temporary breakdown of the machine, which caused a delay too great to be subsequently made up. Mr. Cooper's characteristic recollection of the event, as given fifty-five years later, was that "they tried a little race one day, but it didn't amount to anything. It was rather funny; and the locomotive got out of gear." [49]

Mr. Latrobe says of the Tom Thumb:—

"The machine was not larger than the hand cars used by workmen to transfer themselves from place to place; and as the speaker now recalls its appearance, the only wonder is that so apparently insignificant a contrivance should ever have been regarded as competent to the smallest results. But Mr. Cooper was wiser than many of the wisest around him. His engine could not have weighed a ton; but he saw in it a principle which the forty-ton engines of to-day have but served to develop and demonstrate. The boiler of Mr. Cooper's engine was not as large as the kitchen boiler attached to many a range in modern mansions. It was of about the same diameter, but not much more than half as high. It stood upright in the car, and was filled above the furnace, which occupied the lower section, with vertical tubes. The cylinder was but three and one half inches in diameter; and speed was got up by gearing. No natural draft could have been sufficient to get up steam in so small a boiler; and Mr. Cooper used, [50] therefore, a blowing apparatus, driven by a drum, attached to one of the car wheels, over which passed a cord, that, in its turn, worked a pulley on the shaft of the blower. The contrivance for dispensing with a crank, though its general appearance is recollected, the speaker cannot describe with any accuracy; nor is it important,—it came to nothing. . . .

"In a patent case, tried many years afterwards, the boiler of Mr. Cooper's engine became, in some connection which has been forgotten, important as a piece of evidence. It was hunted for, and found among some old rubbish at Mount Clare. It was difficult to imagine that it had even generated steam enough to drive a coffee mill, much less that it had performed the feats here narrated."

After this experimental demonstration, the Tom Thumb retired into honorable but obscure repose in its maker's warehouse at New York, from which it emerged, fifty years later, to take part in the centennial celebration of the beginning of the commercial [51] history of Baltimore (that place having been made a port of entry in 1780). According to a contemporary report of the festival, "in the vast procession, Mr. Cooper and his little Tom Thumb locomotive were the two most conspicuous objects, and received all the honors which could be paid by a quarter of a million of enthusiastic people."

[52]

VI

MUNICIPAL AFFAIRS

Peter Cooper's acquaintance with the affairs of New York city ranged from the time when, as a child, he was taken by his mother to see the last remaining fragments of the stockade erected by the early inhabitants for protection against the Indians, to the full metropolitan glory of the decade of his death. This wonderful municipal history is too commonly regarded from a special standpoint, as if it were but the record of a continually renewed and often unsuccessful struggle against corrupt and incompetent city government. Contests of this kind, under democratic institutions, always occupy more space in the press, and make more noise in public oratory, than the quiet but steady progress of commercial undertakings, and the labors of unselfish citizens for education, art, and social improvement, which go [53] on beneath the turbulent surface. Americans have long suffered under the unjust imputation of peculiar devotion to "the almighty dollar." The fact is that in no other country do individuals give so much or do so much without pecuniary reward—whether for personal friendship or for public spirit—as in the United States. The munificence of private benefactions and endowments, far surpassing the government support given in other nations to similar institutions, furnish an abundant proof of the first half of this proposition; while the other half is proved by the innumerable boards, committees, and other organized bodies, to which active business men give time and thought without remuneration.

This spirit has never been wholly missed in public affairs, even in the city of New York, so often charged with the lack of it. All the great features of its municipal progress, even those which have been, at some stage, tainted with lamentable corruption, have been originated or supported by unselfish public spirit. It might even be said [54] that without this support, innocently given and deceitfully misused, the schemers for private gain could not have achieved their periodical and temporary successes.

Peter Cooper was an illustrious example of good citizenship in this respect. First elected to public office as "assistant alderman," in 1828, he turned his attention immediately upon the subject most important to the growth and welfare of a city, yet most likely to be neglected until it is forced upon the community as an unwelcome necessity,—namely, the water supply. Up to that time, New York had depended upon the springs of Manhattan Island, some of which supplied water, conveyed through the streets by means of wooden pipes (bored logs), while most of them were utilized by means of pumps only, to which the inhabitants sent for their supply. [6]

[55]

Mr. Cooper induced the water committee, of which he had been appointed a member, to visit Philadelphia and inspect the works by which the water of the Schuylkill was raised to a high reservoir, and thence distributed in iron pipes throughout that city, and then to examine the Croton and Bronx rivers, for the purpose of ascertaining what these streams could supply. The season being dry, the rivers were so low that Mr. Cooper was not satisfied of their capacity to furnish the needed quantity; so he investigated further, on his own account, the watershed (then a wilderness) of the Hackensack River in New Jersey, and subsequently [56] submitted to the board of aldermen plans and models, illustrating a scheme for the supply of water to New York from that region, by means of pipes laid under the North River.

To the end of his life, Mr. Cooper adhered to his preference for this method of conveying water across river channels, as compared with elevated aqueducts, like the "high bridge" subsequently constructed across the Harlem River. And in this particular, his intuitive engineer's judgment was not at fault, although the classic example of the Romans, who spent untold labor and time in building aqueducts, where buried conduits would have been both cheaper and better, still dominated the professional world. But Peter Cooper furnished another example of his practical wisdom, by sacrificing his superior theory for the sake of the useful result contemplated. Thorough study showed that, although the Croton region could not be relied upon at all times for an immediately adequate water supply, yet its average through the year was sufficient for [57] the purpose, so that the creation, by means of higher dams, of large storage reservoirs, would solve the pressing problem. This plan was ultimately adopted, and has been pursued with suitable enlargements, ever since. Peter Cooper was made chairman of the water committee,—a position which he retained until some years after the Croton system was completed.

In the procurement of iron pipes for the system of distribution, and their proper testing before acceptance, his integrity and intelligence were specially effective in protecting the interests of the city, by securing the best material at the lowest cost. While Mr. Cooper was a strong "protectionist," favoring the encouragement of American industries, he never recognized any distinctions among Americans. In his patriotic thought, the unit to be regarded was not the city or the State of New York, but the United States of America; and he earnestly opposed the contention of the New York iron founders, that contracts for the pipe of the Croton system ought not to be made with inhabitants [58] of another State. His arguments prevailed; and the pipe was ordered from a Philadelphia manufacturer, who offered a better article at a lower price.

During Mr. Cooper's official service, and not without his active aid and advice (though his personal attention was mainly given to the water department), the beginnings of an organized police and fire service were established. When he was first elected to office the city was guarded by watchmen, who served four hours every night for seventy-five cents. Every householder was expected to have leathern buckets in his hall, and in case of an alarm of fire to throw them into the street, so that the citizens voluntarily running to the rescue could form a line to the nearest pump, and, passing the water by means of the buckets, supply the tank of the small hand-engine, which then squirted it upon the burning building. It is needless to detail here the steps by which out of this crude beginning the present effective New York Fire Department has been perfected. Suffice it to say that the beginning itself was [59] promoted, and its future importance was foreseen, by Peter Cooper and his public-spirited colleagues.

But a still more profoundly important element of municipal and national progress, in which the participation of Peter Cooper was active and influential, was the free public school system in New York. This system was originally planted by the great mayor and governor, De Witt Clinton, to whom the State is indebted for the Erie Canal, and for many other plans and impulses scarcely less significant. While Clinton was an advocate of universal suffrage, he perceived the danger of granting this power to an ignorant and largely foreign population; and in 1805 he secured a charter for "The Society for Establishing a Free School in the City of New York for the Education of Such Poor Children as do not Belong to, or are not Provided for by, Any Religious Society."

The appeal of this society to "the affluent and charitable of every denomination of Christians" was liberally answered, and by [60] December, 1809, a school capable of accommodating five hundred children had been erected upon a purchased site. This was the beginning in New York city of the free school system, over which for twenty-five years De Witt Clinton presided. During that period the schools, supported by generous private contributions, and also after a while by a state tax, steadily increased in number, efficiency, and public favor. Peter Cooper had been always a zealous supporter of these schools, but not until 1838 did he become—by election as a trustee of the Free School Society—officially connected with them. It was a critical period in their history. The original national debt of the Union had been recently extinguished, and a considerable surplus had been returned to the contributing States, of which New York devoted its share to educational purposes, thus largely increasing the fund for the city. In 1822, sixteen years before, the common council had made the free schools "unsectarian," excluding from the benefits of the fund all institutions of denominational character. [61] The various sects had submitted reluctantly to this decision so long as the fund was too small to be divided among them; but its sudden enlargement encouraged an attempt to secure appropriations for parochial schools.

In his first annual message Governor Seward recommended to the legislature the establishment of schools in which the children of foreigners might be "instructed by teachers speaking the same language with themselves and professing the same faith." The Roman Catholic community, acting at once upon this suggestion, sent a deputation to the New York common council demanding for their schools "a pro rata share" of the educational fund, to which as taxpayers they contributed.

In the resistance made to this claim by the Free School Society Mr. Cooper took a prominent and ardent part. The advocates of unsectarian public schools were victorious; but the controversy continued to agitate the State until the passage by the legislature in 1842 of an act establishing in New York [62] city a new board of education to control the schools supported from the funds of the State, and at the same time forbidding the support from this fund of schools in which "any religious sectarian doctrine or tenet shall be taught, inculcated, or practiced." The Free School Society, resenting and distrusting this new (and in some respects complicated) arrangement, continued its separate activity for eleven years; but in 1853, the unsectarian character of the public schools of New York having been established beyond question, the society and the board of education were by common consent amalgamated by statute. At the final meeting of the society Peter Cooper delivered the valedictory address, the language of which indicates that not without apprehension did he contemplate the surrender of the public schools to the exclusive control of a body of officials likely to be more or less influenced by partisan or political considerations.

Yet his characteristic common sense came again in this instance to the front. The [63] moral which he drew from his doubts and fears was that "the stewardship we are about to resign is not a reprieve from the responsibilities of the future." And in obedience to this conviction he accepted, with fourteen of his old colleagues, membership in the board of education, of which he served for two years as vice-president, resigning in January, 1855, at which time he had formed and begun to carry out the great plan of an institution for free popular education with which his name is now forever associated.

Many years later Mr. Cooper became the president of the Citizens' Association of New York, which he supported with untiring enthusiasm and lavish expenditure, and which in its day did good work in securing for the city an efficient fire department, boards of health, docks, and education, and an improved charter. Mr. Cooper retired in 1873, and the association died soon after, to be revived in other organizations, which have from time to time continued the perennial battle for good government in New York begun by him.

[64]

VII

THE COOPER UNION FOR THE ADVANCEMENT OF SCIENCE AND ART

In many respects the industrial conditions under which Peter Cooper began his career had been revolutionized before he finished it. The apprentice system has well-nigh passed away; and the old freedom with which an intelligent, industrious, and ambitious young man could turn from one occupation to another, seeking that road which offered greatest promise of preferment, is greatly hampered by the modern regime of "organized labor," which, whatever its advantages, presents its own peculiar perils for the workingman. But it remains forever true that under either of these systems, or any others that can be evolved or invented, knowledge is power, and the bestowal of it is the one gift which neither pauperizes the recipient nor injures the community. [65]

As a struggling young apprentice, Peter Cooper regarded with intense sympathy the needs and limitations of the class to which he belonged. But his notion of a remedy was not that of paternal legislation, or belligerent organization, or social reconstruction. To his conception the atmosphere of personal liberty and responsibility furnished by the new democratic republic, offering free scope to individual endeavor and rewarding individual merit, was the best that could be asked.

What he dreamed of doing was simply to assist these social conditions by providing for those who were handicapped by circumstances the means of power and opportunity, to be utilized by their own assiduity. This plan included not only what he then thought to be the most effective system for intellectual improvement, but also provision for such innocent entertainment as would supersede the grosser forms of recreation, which involved the waste of money and health.

Walking up the Bowery Road—then the [66] stage route to Boston, but now a crowded down-town street—he selected in the suburbs of the city the site for his great institution; and, as he accumulated the necessary funds, he bought at intervals lot after lot at the intersection of Third and Fourth Avenues, until he had acquired the entire block, paying for his latest purchases (made after the neighborhood had been solidly built up and had become a centre of business) very high prices compared with those he had paid at the beginning. At last (in 1854) he commenced the erection of a six-story fire-proof building of stone, brick, and iron. This work occupied several years, and during its progress a period of great financial distress threatened to interrupt it. But he persisted in the undertaking, at great risk to his private business; and the building was finished at a cost (including that of the land) of more than six hundred and thirty thousand dollars. Subsequent gifts from Mr. Cooper, together with the legacy provided by his will, and doubled by his heirs, and still later donations from his family and immediate [67] relatives, make up a total of more than double that amount. [7]

[68]

Up to the time when the building was completed Mr. Cooper had taken little advice as to the details of his project. Its outlines in his mind were those which he had conceived a quarter-century before, and though he was doubtless conscious that new social and industrial conditions had intervened which would require some modifications of his plan, he had not formulated such changes.

The classes which he wished especially to reach were those who, being already engaged in earning a living by labor, could scarcely be expected to take regular courses in instruction; and the idea of such instruction appears to have been at the beginning subordinate in his mind. He had a strong impression that young mechanics and apprentices, instead of wasting their time in dissipation, should improve their minds during the intervals of labor; and not unnaturally his first thought as to the means of such improvement turned to those things [69] which had aroused and stimulated his own mind. Probably he did not realize that the mass of men were not like himself, and that something more than mere suggestion or opportunity would be required to develop the mental powers and enlarge the knowledge of the average workingman. However that may be, the original vague design of Mr. Cooper was something like this:—

There was in the city of New York a famous collection of curiosities known as Scudder's Museum. Barnum's Museum afterwards took its place; but that, too, has long since disappeared; and the small so-called museums now scattered through the city but faintly remind old inhabitants of the glories of Scudder's or Barnum's in their prime. These establishments contained all sorts of curiosities, arranged without much reference to scientific use,—wax-works, historical relics, dwarfs, giants, living and stuffed animals, etc. There was also a lecture-room, devoted principally to moral melodrama; and on an upper floor a large room was occupied by the cosmorama,—an [70] exhibition of pictures, usually of noteworthy scenery, foreign cities, etc., which were looked at through round holes, enhancing the effect of their illumination.

Peter Cooper doubtless often lingered in these museums, receiving the inspiration which came from visions of a world much wider than his individual horizon, from the curious and wonderful works of nature, and from the works of man in former times and in foreign lands. From the queer mechanical devices exhibited by inventors to the "Happy Family" and the cosmorama, everything was full to his quick sympathy of intellectual, moral, or sentimental suggestion;

and no doubt he felt, after an hour of such combined wonder and reflection, a satisfying sense of time well spent.

He wished that this means of mental improvement and recreation combined might be freely afforded to those whose scanty earnings would not permit them otherwise to make frequent use of it, and he resolved that the museum and the cosmorama should be included in his institution. [71]

Another agency of which Mr. Cooper had made fruitful use, and the efficacy of which he highly appreciated, was conversation and debate. If people could be brought together and made to talk he thought they would learn a great deal from each other. In this he had undoubtedly grasped one of the great principles of progress. To meet and interchange our ideas of books and by personal discussions is indeed the mightiest factor of modern improvement. But the mere meeting to talk *about* things unless it is combined with the disposition and the apparatus for *studying* things is but barter without production, and may degenerate to a barren exchange of words, as unprofitable as that described in the Yankee proverb, "swapping jackknives in a garret." This aspect of the truth Mr. Cooper doubtless came to appreciate; but at the outset, habituated as he was to get ideas from everybody he met and everything he saw, it seemed to him that free discussions would be an unmixed benefit to all, and he resolved that his institution should contain rooms, devoted to the several [72] handicrafts, where the practitioners of each could meet and "exchange views."

It was also his intention that the lower part of the building he erected should be occupied by stores and offices, the annual rent of which should pay the running expenses of the institution. In the course of time the Cooper Union came to need for full efficiency both more money than this source would supply and more room than was left to it after subtracting the rooms thus rented. These needs have now been met in some measure by further endowments, so that before long the whole building will be devoted to educational uses. But the wisdom, at that time, of Mr. Cooper's plan has been vindicated by the great work done with the modest means thus provided.

The building of the Cooper Union represented his original ideas. Above the shops and offices to be rented was an immense room intended for the museum. A large part of the building was cut up into small meeting-rooms for the conferences of the trades; in an upper story another great [73] room was provided for the cosmorama; and the flat roof was to be safely inclosed with a balustrade, so that on pleasant days or evenings the frequenters of the institution might sit or promenade there, partake of harmless refreshments, listen to agreeable music, [8] and enjoy the magnificent prospect of the city below,—the heights beyond the East River on one side, the Hudson on the other, and the magnificent island-studded harbor.

A noteworthy feature of this scheme was the complete obliteration of all distinctions of class, creed, race, or sex among its beneficiaries. It is a significant fact that through nearly half a century, while these distinctions have been the subjects of vehement and sometimes bitter social and political discussion, the Cooper Union has gone quietly on educating its thousands of pupils without the least embarrassment in its discipline, and apparently without even the consciousness on the part of its founder or its trustees that in this [74] perfect solution of what was supposed to be a difficult problem they had accomplished anything extraordinary.

When Mr. Cooper, consulting with wise and practical advisers, addressed himself at last to the final arrangement of details, he surrendered one after another many parts of his youthful design. The name, "The Cooper Union for the Advancement of Science and Art," epitomized this change. His primary purpose was unchanged; but he perceived that systematic education would be of more value to the class he sought to aid than mere amusement or miscellaneous talk. The great free reading-room of the Cooper Union was substituted for the museum; the conversation parlors for the various trades became class-rooms for instruction; the cosmorama yielded to lecture-halls and laboratories; and the roof was abandoned to the weather. To all these changes, and to many other novelties adopted afterwards, Mr. Cooper was reconciled by one conclusive argument; namely, the proof afforded by their results that the Cooper Union was giving to the working [75] classes that which they needed most and most desired. Now and then perhaps a sigh might escape him for the dream of his youth. I remember one occasion when I accompanied him to the roof of the building, where some new construction was going on which he wished to inspect. The old man stood for some time admiring the view in all directions, and at last, recalling how he had once imagined happy crowds enjoying the delights of that "roof-garden," and casting a mournful glance at the central spot where the band was to have been, he said, "Sometimes I think my first plan was the best!" [9] But such regrets did not occupy his mind. He [76] was satisfied to know that the institution he had founded, building better than he knew, had proved its fitness by its success in the eager and grateful use made of it by those for whose benefit it was intended and in the actual evidences of such benefit. Every year managers of the different departments took pains to report to him instances in which students already earning wages had increased their earnings through the added knowledge or skill acquired in the evening classes; and this was the feature of the annual statements upon which he dwelt with the greatest satisfaction.

[77]

The charter of the Cooper Union was finally adopted in its present form by the legislature of the State of New York, April 13, 1859; and the deed of trust, executed in compliance therewith, on the 29th day of the same month, by Peter Cooper and his wife, Sarah, conveyed to the board of trustees the title to "all that piece and parcel of land bounded on the west by Fourth Avenue, on the north by Astor Place, on the east by Third Avenue, and on the south by Seventh Street, . . . to be forever devoted to the advancement of science and art, in their application to the varied and useful purposes of life."

Even through this dry legal phraseology, it is not difficult to discern the frank and simple joy of the patient enthusiast, who was at last able to speak of the land which he had laboriously acquired, lot by lot, through many years, and the building which he had raised, stone by stone, through many more, as *one* "piece or parcel," his to dedicate forever.

The delivery of this deed to the board of [78] trustees was accompanied with a long letter, setting forth the wishes, hopes, and plans of the grantor, in the formal and diffuse rhetoric peculiar to his generation, and, perhaps, too much contemned by ours. To say the least, we are no more warranted in despising the utterances of noble, self-sacrificing philanthropists, because they are clothed in phrases now deemed verbose and stilted, than we would be in disparaging the deeds of historic heroes, because they wore armor now antiquated and struck their doughty blows with weapons obsolete. When Peter Cooper wrote, in the letter now before me, "The great object I desire to accomplish by the establishment of an institution devoted to the advancement of science and art is to open the volume of nature by the light of truth—so unveiling the laws and methods of Deity that the young may see the beauties of creation, enjoy its blessings, and learn to love the Being 'from whom cometh every good and perfect gift,'"—he was not guilty of cant, because cant is the use of language expressing an emotion which the user does [79] not really feel. And the same may be said of the elaborate additional exposition, contained in this letter, of the writer's faith in God and man, and of his confident hope in the future of his race, and particularly of his country.

The letter shows some traces still of his original plan. Thus, he writes:—

"In order most effectually to aid and encourage the efforts of youth to obtain useful knowledge, I have provided the main floor of the large hall on the third story for a reading-room, literary exchange, and scientific collections—the walls around that floor to be arranged for the reception of books, maps, paintings, and other objects of interest. And when a sufficient collection of the works of art, science, and nature can be obtained, I propose that glass cases shall be arranged around the walls of the gallery of the said room, forming alcoves around the entire floor for the preservation of the same. In the window spaces I propose to arrange such cosmoramic and other views as will exhibit in the clearest and most forcible light the true philosophy of life." [80]

Other characteristic paragraphs are here quoted,—the whole letter being too long for full republication.

"To manifest the deep interest and sympathy I feel in all that can advance the happiness and better the condition of the female portion of the community, and especially of those who are dependent on honest labor for support, I desire the trustees to appropriate two hundred and fifty dollars yearly to assist such pupils of the female school of design as shall, in their careful judgment, by their efforts and sacrifices in the performance of duty to parents or to those that Providence has made dependent on them for support, merit and require such aid. My reason for this requirement is not so much to reward as to encourage the exercise of heroic virtues that often shine in the midst of the greatest suffering and obscurity without so much as being noticed by the passing throng.

"In order to better the condition of women and to widen the sphere of female employment, I have provided seven rooms to [81] be forever devoted to a female school of design, and I desire the trustees to appropriate out of the rents of the building fifteen hundred dollars annually towards meeting the expenses of said school.

"It is the ardent wish of my heart that this school of design may be the means of raising to competence and comfort thousands of those that might otherwise struggle through a life of poverty and suffering. . . .

"Desiring, as I do, to use every means to render this institution useful through all coming time, and believing that editors of the public press have it in their power to exert a greater influence on the community for good than any other class of men of equal number, it is therefore my sincere desire that editors be earnestly invited to become members of the society of arts to be connected with this institution. . . .

"It is my desire, also, that the students shall have the use of one of the large rooms (to be assigned by the trustees) for the purpose of useful debates. I desire and deem it best to direct that all these lectures and [82] debates shall be exclusive of theological and party questions, and shall have for their constant object the causes that operate around and within us, and the means necessary and most appropriate to remove the physical and moral evils that afflict our city, our country, and humanity." . . .

Other paragraphs indicate his plan that the students shall, in the first instance, frame the rules which shall control the discipline of the institution. Thus he says:—

"It is my desire, and I hereby ordain, that a strict conformity to rules deliberately formed by a vote of the majority of the students, and approved by the trustees, shall forever be an indispensable requisite for continuing to enjoy the benefits of this institution. I now most earnestly entreat each and every one of the students of this institution, through all coming time, to whom I have intrusted this great responsibility of framing laws for the regulation of their conduct in their connection with the institution, and by which any of the members may lose its privileges, to remember how frail we are, [83] and how liable to err when we come to sit in judgment on the faults of others, and how much the circumstances of our birth, our education, and the society and country where we have been born and brought up, have had to do in forming us and making us what we are."

In this scheme Mr. Cooper anticipated the plan of self-government now followed in some of our colleges; and while he expected too much of the students of the Cooper Union, and was himself afterwards obliged to consent to the restriction of their autonomy, it may be fairly said that the spirit of his hope and exhortation has never ceased to be felt; and, to the great honor of the Cooper Union, it may be recorded that questions of discipline have been well-nigh unknown within its walls.

This noble trust was accepted by a body of men who have discharged it with unwearied fidelity, zeal and wisdom. The original board consisted of Mr. Cooper, his son Edward Cooper, his son-in-law Abram S. Hewitt, and John E. Parsons, Wilson G. [84] Hunt, and Daniel F. Tiemann. Three of these, Messrs. Cooper, Hewitt, and Tiemann, have been mayors of the city of New York. All of them were well-known and eminent citizens, burdened with the duties of active business; and the time they gave so freely to the management of the Cooper Union was not the superfluity of leisure. The difficulty with "business men" too often is, that, when nominally charged with the administration of organized charities, they slight the work because they have not time to attend to it. But the United States can show not a few instances in which the affairs of religious, educational, or benevolent institutions are carefully managed by the active directors of great private enterprises; and their management, when it is thus thorough, is generally much better than that of literary or philanthropic amateurs. This is conspicuously shown in the history of the Cooper Union. [10]

[85]

This is not the place for a detailed account of the development of the Cooper Union, or even of its present scope and prospective operations. Such an account would worthily occupy a separate volume; for the institution, in the hands of its wise directors, was a pioneer and model in many respects in which later enterprises, with larger means, have, perhaps, surpassed it. I must content myself here with brief mention of a few particulars.

The immense free reading-room, with its average daily attendance of nearly 1500 to 2000 persons, was Mr. Cooper's special delight; and well it might be so; for the sight is one almost without a parallel—not in the architecture, size, or furnishing of the place, but in the extent and constancy of its use by the public. Entrance is free to all who are not unclean, intoxicated, or disorderly. In the main, the privileges thus given are not abused, but occasionally the evils almost inseparable from so large an attendance have been felt. At one time, the curator earnestly represented to the trustees the necessity [86] of doing something to check the mutilation of books—a practice which public librarians know well as one of their most troublesome foes. It appeared that some unknown persons, who combined a love of the beautiful in language with a barbaric ignorance of it in conduct, were accustomed to slash out with their penknives favorite passages of poetry for preservation, treating in this matter newspapers and books alike. It was found difficult to keep whole the volumes of Tennyson and Longfellow. But a more frequent and injurious practice was the cutting out of plates from illustrated books. This was not for love of art, as the other for love of poetry. The object was to sell such engravings for two or three cents each to the print-shops in the city, where they were bought by refined amateurs, for the purpose of "illustrating" special volumes. This fashionable hobby has been the indirect cause of the ruin of many a choice book; and buyers of fine old editions are well aware that they must look well to their bargains, lest they find that the thief, at the bidding [87] of the "collector," has plundered the volumes of the plates which once adorned them.

When this subject came up for discussion in the board of trustees, Mr. Cooper was so full of pity for the poor fellows, who were obliged to sell stolen engravings at two cents a piece to keep body and soul together, that he could scarcely be brought to take a severe view of the offense. Nor was he willing (and in this his fellow-trustees agreed with him) to impose any restriction or censorship upon admittance to the reading-room. Even if the books suffered, the room must continue to be free. The great mass of well-behaved people must not be annoyed by measures intended to exclude a few rogues. The result vindicated the sagacity, as well as the charity, of this view. The officers in charge, not being permitted to adopt any sweeping measures of prevention, simply redoubled their vigilance, and finally caught one or two offenders and "made examples of them;" and the nuisance was immediately abated, though perhaps not entirely and permanently abolished. [88]

The report of 1900, after mentioning the great (legitimate) wear and tear of the books, of which 12,000 had to be re-bound, adds:—

"The decorum of the visitors has been excellent, and it is remarkable, in view of such a very large number of persons visiting the room, that so few mutilations and injuries occur to the periodicals and books, and that so few books, probably not more than half a dozen in the course of a year, and those of small consequence, are stolen."

It seems then, after all, that Peter Cooper's faith in the people was justified.

The great hall in the basement is another noteworthy feature, and worthy of wider imitation than it has yet received. Such a hall, if located upstairs in such a building, would have been open to three objections: it would have monopolized, for occasional use only, space which was required for constant use; it would have been intolerably noisy, by reason of the roar and rattle in the streets which surround the building on all sides; and it would have been [89] dangerous, as all such places are, when great audiences must make their exit by going down stairs. Nothing has ever been invented that will prevent people from being crushed and trampled when they are crowding down a stairway. In all these respects, the great hall of the Cooper Union is admirable. It occupies space not otherwise valuable. It is quiet, and acoustically perfect. The means of exit and entrance are ample and safe. Even in case of an unreasoning panic, there is little danger that a crowd, tumbling up the stone stairways to the street, would cause the horrible maiming and killing which so often attend the efforts of a frightened multitude to get down. Finally, the ventilation is excellent, for the simple reason that natural or automatic ventilation of such a large, low basement room could not be expected, and consequently mechanical ventilation by means of a large fan, run by steam power, was provided. The efficiency of this system has sometimes been severely tested. On one occasion, during a scientific lecture, the experimental illustrations [90] of which were on a large and imposing scale, the learned professor on the platform had the misfortune to crack an immense glass jar, in which he was exhibiting the brilliant combustion of phosphorus in oxygen gas. The white fumes of phosphorous acid floated out into the air, and began to diffuse themselves through the hall towards the ventilation outlets at the sides and rear. To one who knew the irritating nature of these fumes it seemed inevitable that the hall must be emptied of its crowded audience in a few minutes. Already coughing had begun on the front seats, when Mr. Hewitt, who was seated on the platform, quickly rose, and pulling a cord, reversed the currents of ventilation and opened a new outlet into the street, behind and above the platform. The curling clouds of vapor paused, wheeled, and retreated, and in another minute the air was perfectly pure. The lecturer had not even been interrupted. It was a beautiful and timely "experiment" not on the programme, and, to use the words of one who was present, "It was just the [91] sort of thing to please Peter Cooper to the bottom of his soul."

The great hall was dedicated from the beginning to free speech. Peter Cooper may have overestimated the value of mere talk. As I have already told, it was his first notion that conversation and discussion were the chief things required in education. He came to see that study, instruction, and training were equally essential, but he never surrendered his faith in free speech; and the great hall was at the service of all sects, parties, and classes, religious, philosophical, political, scientific, literary, or philanthropic. It has been the scene of many memorable meetings and addresses. But nothing in its history has been more useful and noteworthy than the series of free popular lectures which were given, as part of the operations of the Cooper Union, within its walls. These lectures began in 1868, and continued until they were adopted by the city as part of the general scheme of free lectures which has been so successful during the last few years. In awarding due praise to the promoters [92] and managers of this plan, it should not be forgotten that the Cooper Union inaugurated it, and maintained it for many years, during which the free Saturday night popular lectures in its great hall were the only ones of their kind. They covered many sciences and arts, chronicles of travel and themes of history and literature. The most eminent authors, teachers, investigators, travelers, and orators of the generation were comprised in the list of lecturers; and many of them performed this service without other reward than the consciousness of contributing to a noble charity, and the evident gratitude of the vast and eagerly attentive audience.

Mr. Cooper loved to attend these Saturday evening lectures, and an arm-chair was always ready for him on the platform. Many a speaker on that platform has been surprised by an untimely outburst of applause and has turned to discover the cause in the entrance of the beloved founder. Often the subject of the evening was beyond his experience or knowledge, but that made no difference in his respectful attention, or in [93] the benign satisfaction with which he contemplated the attentive audience, and realized that they were receiving benefit. I have often felt that the scene exhibited almost every Saturday night for many years during the latest period of his life could be equaled only by the spectacle presented at Ephesus, where the aged St. John the Divine fronted the congregation of loving believers, always with his one last message, "Little children, love one another."

But sometimes the old man would be intensely interested and aroused by the lecture. I remember such an occasion, when I was myself the lecturer, and had been laying down, with due scientific decorum and diagrams, the "law of storms." At the close of the lecture, Mr. Cooper arose, advanced to the front, and gave a vivid and animated description of a whirlwind which he had witnessed some seventy years before, which was received with rapt attention and tremendous applause. The lecture was undoubtedly eclipsed in interest by this unexpected after-piece; but the lecturer was amply

[94] compensated by his triumph in having thus stirred the spirit and aroused the recollections of the dear old founder.

With regard to the various schools and classes of the Cooper Union, it must suffice to say briefly that under the elastic and comprehensive plan of the deed of trust, two objects were constantly kept in view by the trustees. In the first place, a complete four years' course was always maintained, for the benefit of those who could afford the time and who felt the need of such training. In the second place, classes were instituted in such special departments as were most likely to be useful and most evidently in demand; and with regard to these the demand and the evidence of usefulness were followed as guides in determining the extent of the facilities offered, up to the capacity and means of the institution.

De Morgan, in his "Budget of Paradoxes," tells of an old fellow who, wishing to have a chair that would fit him perfectly, sat for a while on a mass of shoemaker's wax, which he then carried to a worker in [95] wood, and instructed him to "make a seat like that!" This homely illustration indicates the manner in which the special classes of the Cooper Union have been established, enlarged, and regulated, to meet the evident demands of its constituency. It is pleasant to know that the future means and sphere of the institution will be enlarged under the same wise management.

[96]

VIII

NATIONAL POLITICS

Peter Cooper's prominent activity in national politics belongs to two periods,—that of the war for the Union, and that of the subsequent controversies over questions of financial policy.

As has been explained, he felt his life to be peculiarly identified with that of the nation born with him; and the idea that this nation should be destroyed in the midst of its triumphant progress was profoundly abhorrent to him. Like many other patriots, he was ready to save the Union by a compromise, if that were practicable.

He advocated the purchase and liberation by the government of all the slaves in the United States; he promoted a "peace conference" on the very eve of the war. But when South Carolina had formally seceded and the gauntlet had [97] been cast at the feet of national authority, his course was not uncertain. He was a representative of the New York Chamber of Commerce in the deputation of thirty leading citizens of New York which visited Washington in order to discover what plan Mr. Buchanan (then still President) had in view. They got no satisfaction from the President, but assured themselves of the firm loyalty of Mr. Seward, then Senator from New York.

A few weeks later the bombardment of Fort Sumter put an end to all projects of compromise. At the memorable mass meeting held in Union Square, New York, shortly after the receipt of this news, Peter Cooper, then seventy years old, was among the first to mount the platform. His familiar white hairs and kindly face were recognized by the crowd, which vociferously called for a speech from him. Stepping to the front, he uttered a few ringing sentences which sounded the keynote of the meeting. I quote but one or two:—

"We are contending with an enemy not [98] only determined on our destruction as a nation, but to build on our ruins a government devoted with all its power to maintain, extend, and perpetuate a system in itself revolting to all the best feelings of humanity,—an institution that enables thousands to sell their own children into hopeless bondage.

"Shall it succeed? You say 'No!' and I unite with you in your decision. We cannot allow it to succeed. We should spend our lives, our property, and leave the land itself a desolation before such an institution should triumph over the free people of this country. . . .

"Let us, therefore, unite to sustain the government by every means in our power, to arm and equip in the shortest possible time an army of the best men that can be found in the country."

From that day on his patriotism never doubted or faltered. When the war loan was announced he was the first man at the door of the subtreasury in New York waiting to make payment over the counter of [99] all the money he had been able to collect without business disaster. "In those days," says a friend, "whenever he had nothing else to do, he would go down to the recruiting office and put in a substitute." It is estimated that he must have sent, first and last, about a score of soldiers to serve for him under the flag.

From the first he urged the emancipation and enlistment of the Southern negroes,—a policy which was ultimately adopted with successful results; and when in 1864, at the darkest hour of the struggle, there was danger of a fatal compromise, he actively promoted that great mass meeting in the hall of the Cooper Union which marked the turning-point of the struggle, carried the State of New York for Lincoln, and secured the triumph of the Union.

After the war was over he presided at another meeting, called to favor aid to the disabled soldiers of the nation; and the following paragraph quoted from his remarks on that occasion forms a fitting close to this brief notice of his patriotic activity: [100] —

"If we required a stronger stimulus to urge us to perform our duty, we have only to turn our thoughts back to that fearful day when the armies of rebellion had entered Pennsylvania with the intent to subjugate the North to their domination. Had they been successful, they would have gloried in making us pay for the loss of their slaves and the expenses of their war. I trust that the government will not hesitate to tax my property and the property of every other man enough to provide for the comfort of our disabled soldiers and the families dependent on them for support."

In the financial controversies which accompanied and followed the period of "reconstruction" after the war, and were involved in the payment and adjustment of the national debt, Mr. Cooper appeared as an advocate of the "Greenback" party, and did not seem to realize that this was a complete reversal of his earlier position as a "hard-money" Democrat. I think the clue to this change may be found in his recollection of the war waged by Andrew Jackson on the [101] United States Bank, and a vague feeling that the national banking system instituted by Secretary Chase was open to similar objections. To this may be added his growing inclination in favor of "paternal government,"—which in a man so thoroughly self-supporting and self-reliant can be explained only by the fact that his personal philanthropy overbalanced his political philosophy; that he became more anxious to relieve the distress he saw than to question the wisdom of measures taken for that purpose. Two things are certain: first, that Mr. Cooper's motives in his later political course were thoroughly pure and unselfish; and secondly, that his utterances and publications in this connection show him to be dealing with subjects which he did not understand. This statement is made without regard to the merits of the controversy, or the strength of the arguments contributed to it by others. The simple truth is that Mr. Cooper was too old to make original investigation of such questions, intelligently weighing all the modern conditions of industry [102] and commerce, in which he was no longer an active participant. He accepted in 1876 the nomination of the Greenback party for the presidency; but the issue was already practically dead, and he received but 81,740 votes out of a total of 8,412,833 cast. Undaunted by this defeat, he continued to utter his views. Those who wish to study them in detail may consult the volume "Ideas for a Science of Good Government in Addresses, Letters, and Articles on a Strictly National Currency, Tariff, and Civil Service," which he issued at the age of ninety-two, in the last year of his life. His own summary of his position, given on page 212 of this book, shows that he desired a national legal-tender paper currency, irredeemable in coin, but "interconvertible" with government bonds, and regulated by law as to volume per capita; a "discriminating" protective tariff, "helpful to all the industries of the country, where the raw material and the labor can be furnished by our own people;" and a civil service divorced from party politics, based on [103] personal fitness, with tenure of office during good behavior, moderate salaries, and pensions for the aged and sick, and provision for widows and orphans.

[104]

IX

THE END

In 1874, at the age of eighty-three, Mr. Cooper said at a reception given in his honor:—

"When I was born, New York contained 27,000 inhabitants. The upper limits of the city were at Chambers Street. Not a single free school, either by day or night, existed. General Washington had just entered upon his first term as President of the United States, the whole annual expenditures of which did not exceed $2,500,000, being about sixty cents per head of the population. Not a single steam engine had yet been built or erected on the American continent; and the people were clad in homespun, and were characterized by the simple virtues and habits which are usually associated with that primitive garb. I need not tell you what the country now is, and what the habits and the garments [105] of its people now are, or that the expenditure, per capita, of the general government has increased fifteen-fold. But I have witnessed and taken a deep interest in every step of the marvellous development and progress which have characterized this century beyond all the centuries which have gone before.

"Measured by the achievements of the years I have seen, I am one of the oldest men who have ever lived; but I do not feel old, and I propose to give you the receipt by which I have preserved my youth.

"I have always given a friendly welcome to new ideas, and I have endeavored not to feel too old to learn; and thus, though I stand here with the snows of so many winters upon my head, my faith in human nature, my belief in the progress of man to a better social condition, and especially my trust in the ability of men to establish and maintain self-government, are as fresh and as young as when I began to travel the path of life.

"While I have always recognized that the object of business is to make money in an [106] honorable manner, I have endeavored to remember that the object of life is to do good. Hence I have been ready to engage in all new enterprises, and, without incurring debt, to risk in their promotion the means which I had acquired, provided they seemed to me calculated to advance the general good. This will account for my early attempt to perfect the steam engine, for my attempt to construct the first American locomotive, for my connection with the telegraph in a course of efforts to unite our country with the European world, and for my recent efforts to solve the problem of economical steam navigation on the canals; to all of which you have so kindly referred. It happens to but few men to change the current of human progress, as it did to Watt, to Fulton, to Stephenson, and to Morse; but most men may be ready to welcome laborers to a new field of usefulness, and to clear the road for their progress.

"This I have tried to do, as well in the perfecting and execution of their ideas as in making such provision as my means have permitted [107] for the proper education of the young mechanics and citizens of my native city, in order to fit them for the reception of new ideas, social, mechanical, and scientific—hoping thus to economize and expand the intellectual as well as the physical forces, and provide a larger fund for distribution among the various classes which necessarily make up the total of society. If our lives shall be such that we shall receive the glad welcome of 'Well done, good and faithful servant,' we shall then know that we have not lived in vain."

For nine years after this utterance he continued the peaceful and happy life which it describes. When the end came, it was quiet and painless. Surrounded by his children and grandchildren, and whispering with almost his last breath the desire for an increase of his bequest to that other well-beloved child, the Cooper Union, he "fell on sleep," April 4, 1883.

On the day of his funeral New York city presented an almost unexampled spectacle. All Soul's Unitarian Church, in which his [108] body was deposited, early in the morning was thronged with a mighty multitude, passing in procession to look upon the beloved face. Eighteen young men from the Cooper Union surrounded it, as a guard of honor. A body of 3500 students of that institution, of both sexes, marched by, casting flowers upon the coffin, and followed by delegations from all the municipal and charitable organizations of the city, and by uncounted multitudes, whose relation to the beloved philanthropist was not official or representative, but simply personal.

The busiest streets of New York, through which the funeral procession passed on its way to Greenwood Cemetery, beyond the East River, were closed to business and hung in black. The flags on all public buildings, and on the ships in the harbor, were at half-mast. The bells of all churches were tolled. The whole city mourned, as it had not done since, eighty years before, the funeral procession of George Washington moved through its streets.

If we seek, without affectionate prejudice, [109] to discover the cause of this universal grief, affection, and admiration, we shall find, I think, that it lies chiefly in two circumstances; namely, the character of Peter Cooper as a lover of his kind, and the opportunity afforded him by his long life, not only to prove that character, but to become personally known to many thousands of those whom he sought unselfishly to serve. Few persons except military commanders have such an opportunity. The philanthropists who labor in secret, no matter with what noble motive, and do not come face to face with their beneficiaries, may win the applause of posterity, but cannot expect to receive the immediate and personal affection of their contemporaries. Least of all do posthumous gifts arouse this sentiment. Peter Cooper, above all other claims to renown and gratitude, identified himself with his philanthropy, and was known where he was loved.

> "Who gives himself with his gift, feeds three:
> Himself, his hungering neighbor, and Me!"

FOOTNOTES:

[1] Many years after his wife's death, and shortly before his own, Mr. Cooper dictated the following passage, which is almost the last in his *Reminiscences:*—

"Not only do I think of my wife during my waking moments; she often comes to me in my dreams, sometimes once a week, sometimes once in two weeks, and sometimes at longer intervals. It is one of the greatest pleasures of my life that I can believe that she has been, and is now, my guardian angel, and it is one of my happiest hopes that I shall see that this our world is but the bud of a being that is to ripen and bear its choicest fruits in another and a better."

[2] Letter of Morse to the Secretary of the Treasury in the autumn of 1843.

[3] These and other statements in this chapter are taken from a lecture, delivered March 23, 1868, before the Maryland Institute, by Hon. J. H. B. Latrobe, giving his personal recollections of the early history of the Baltimore and Ohio Railroad.

[4] Manuscript of his *Reminiscences.*

[5] This was the sacrifice of a favorite invention to immediate practical considerations, which has been mentioned above as an instance of Mr. Cooper's common sense.

[6] A curious survival of this state of things is the Manhattan Company, which secured from the legislature a perpetual charter, so skillfully framed (by Aaron Burr) that, although it grants much more extensive powers than could now be obtained by a corporation, it cannot be successfully assailed so long as the fundamental condition is fulfilled,—namely, that the company shall be prepared to furnish water at all times, on demand. It is said that, in compliance with this requirement, a small steam pump is kept continually running, in connection with a short system of pipes, somewhere near the City Hall, and that the company stands ready to furnish water to any applicant—only, the charter does not fix the price which it may exact! So far as I know, the only use now made of the extensive powers granted by this famous charter is the maintenance

of the Manhattan Bank. A few years ago, excavations in lower Broadway brought to light bored logs, which were supposed to be relics of the old "Manhattan" system.

[7] Not all of this amount is represented in permanent endowments, since large contributions to cover deficits in annual income as compared with current expenses, or for special repairs and alterations, do not appear under that head. According to the balance-sheet of January 1, 1900, the total assets consist of $1,075,428.62, the appraised value of the building, furniture, and apparatus; and $947,021.39 in cash on hand or investments,—making a total of $2,022,450.01. Of the invested sum $953,159.30 is in "special endowments," of which the income only can be expended. This fund comprises $200,000 from Peter Cooper and $340,000 from the family of the late William Cooper, his brother; the remainder is made up of smaller gifts (the chief of which are a bequest of $30,000 from Wilson G. Hunt, one of the original trustees, and $10,000 each from Mary Stuart, J. Pierpont Morgan, Morris K. Jesup, and John E. Parsons), and one of $300,000 made in December, 1899, by Andrew Carnegie. In addition to the aggregate thus made up Hon. Edward Cooper, the son, and Mr. Abram S. Hewitt, the son-in-law of Peter Cooper, have undertaken to furnish a further income of $10,000 per annum; and finally, according to the 41st Annual Report of the Trustees (May, 1900), the Cooper Union, as residuary legatee under the will of the late John Holstead, will ultimately receive between $200,000 and $300,000.

These recent additions to the endowment of the institution will enable the trustees to enlarge its usefulness in many ways, and especially (being no longer dependent for annual income upon rents) to utilize the whole of the building for educational purposes. Yet the total endowment will still be modest, as compared with that of many similar institutions of later origin.

[8] Old New Yorkers will be reminded of the closing lines of Fitz-Greene Halleck's poem,—

> "And there is music twice a week
> On Scudder's balcony."

[9] There may have been more than a mere sentimental regret in his mind at that time; for his inventive intuition had struck out half a century before an idea to which the slow thought of his fellows had not yet attained,—the plan of utilizing roofs for the purpose of giving to all classes an ownership of free air and far distance and boundless sky as complete as any landowner could command by fencing off a mountain for his own pleasure. As he looked down upon the vast wilderness of roofs and thought of the multitude laboring beneath them or trudging through the streets ("up one cañon and down another," as old Jim Bridger the scout said in St. Louis), ignorant of the upper sphere within reach, he might well have felt that one part of his original scheme would still be a physical and moral boon to the metropolis. In fact the disappearance of the "vacant lots," so numerous in his youth, and so freely available as informal parks and playgrounds, had created new necessity for air and space. Whether he consciously recalled the hanging gardens of Babylon, or the flat roofs universally utilized for social and domestic purposes in eastern and southern countries, I do not know. At all events he had seized upon a similar idea, and now nearly a score of years after his death—we are waking up to its value. Even the Cooper Union building some day, after more pressing needs of equipment shall have been satisfied, may be crowned with its garden of rest and outlook.

[10] Of the original board, Peter Cooper was the first to pass away. Mr. Hunt and Mr. Tiemann have since died, and Mr. R. Fulton Cutting has been elected a trustee. The other vacancies have not been filled.